coping with loss

loss

the life changes handbook

Crabtree Publishing Company
www.crabtreebooks.com

Crabtree Publishing Company
www.crabtreebooks.com

Author: Anita Naik
Editor: Molly Aloian
Proofreader: Adrianna Morganelli
Project coordinator: Robert Walker
Production coordinator: Margaret Amy Salter
Prepress technician: Margaret Amy Salter
Project editor: Victoria Garrard
Project designer: Sara Greasley

With thanks to Dr. Melissa Sayer

Every effort has been made to trace copyright holders, and we apologize in advance for any omissions. We would be pleased to insert the appropriate acknowledgments in any subsequent edition of this publication.

Picture credits:

iStockphoto: p. 10, 26, 28, 30, 31

Getty Images: Film Magic: p. 9; Wire Image: p. 11, 29 (bottom)

Sara Greasley and Hayley Terry: front cover (bottom), back cover (bottom), p. 5, 7 (top), 13, 15, 16, 18 (top), 20, 23, 25, 29 (center), 35, 36, 38, 40, 41 (top)

Shutterstock: p. 1, 2, 4, 6, 7 (bottom left and right), 8, 12, 14, 17, 18 (bottom), 19, 22, 24, 27, 29 (top), 32, 34, 37, 39, 41 (center), 42, 45, 47

Ticktock Media Archive: front cover (top), back cover (top)

Library and Archives Canada Cataloguing in Publication

Naik, Anita
  Coping with loss : the life changes handbook / Anita Naik.

(Really useful handbooks)
Includes index.
ISBN 978-0-7787-4391-0 (bound).--ISBN 978-0-7787-4404-7 (pbk.)

  1. Loss (Psychology)--Juvenile literature. 2. Life change events--Juvenile literature. 3. Death--Juvenile literature. 4. Grief--Juvenile literature. 5. Divorce--Juvenile literature. I. Title. II. Series: Really useful handbooks

BF637.C4N33 2009   j155.9'3   C2008-907870-5

Library of Congress Cataloging-in-Publication Data

Naik, Anita.
  Coping with loss : the life changes handbook / Anita Naik.
    p. cm. -- (Really useful handbooks)
  Includes index.
  ISBN 978-0-7787-4404-7 (pbk. : alk. paper) -- ISBN 978-0-7787-4391-0 (reinforced library binding : alk. paper)
  1. Loss (Psychology)--Juvenile literature. 2. Divorce--Juvenile literature. 3. Children and death--Juvenile literature. 4. Grief--Juvenile literature. I. Title. II. Series.

  BF575.D35.N35 2009
  155.9'3083--dc22

2008052370

Crabtree Publishing Company
www.crabtreebooks.com   1-800-387-7650

Published in Canada
Crabtree Publishing
616 Welland Ave.
St. Catharines, Ontario
L2M 5V6

Published in the United States
Crabtree Publishing
PMB16A
350 Fifth Ave., Suite 3308
New York, NY 10118

contents

coping with change

Change can be tough because we like the stability and security of our lives. Change is hard, but change is also necessary. Without it, life wouldn't move forward.

My mom just had a new baby and although he's cute, everything is different and I don't like it.

There's nothing like a new baby to cause a major domestic upheaval. The way to cope with this kind of change is not to think of all the things you have lost but what you've gained. If the feelings of uncertainty won't go away, you need to do three things:

1) Give yourself time to adjust. No one expects you to be happy right away.

2) Talk to your parents about your feelings so they can help you.

3) Think of what you've gained. For example, eventually you'll have someone to help you with the chores.

How to cope with change

Change is hard because it always involves some kind of adjustment. Here's how to cope:

1) **Talk about it.** Discussing your anxieties with friends, family or an older person you trust will help. If you can't find the words, or don't want to talk too anyone, try to keep a diary of your thoughts. This is a great way to alleviate your anxiety.

2) **Prepare for it.** Talk to someone who's been through the same thing or get a book from the library that covers this particular life change. Hearing how others got through it can help you prepare for what's to come.

3) **Give yourself time to handle it.** Time really does heal.

4) **Focus on what you've gained.** For example, you may resent a new sibling at first but they might take the pressure off you and give you more freedom.

5) **Grieve for what you've lost.** It's important not to put on a brave face. Instead allow yourself to feel sad about what you've lost.

6) **Be truthful about your feelings.** If you're not honest about how you feel now, your feelings are only going to resurface at a later date.

It happened to me!

"My parents had another baby when I was 11 years old and I hated it. I wouldn't pick her up or go near her because I was so angry. I liked being the youngest and didn't want a baby sister. Then my older sister said that's how she felt about me when I was born. That was a shock. We're best friends and I never thought she would feel that way about me, so I gave my baby sister a chance and she's not so bad."

Maria, 14

changing schools and friends

I love my old school and don't want to move on.

One of the biggest changes you have to face between the ages of 11 and 16 is changing schools. Sometimes this may be just a change of location. Other times it means making new friends and fitting in all over again.

Give it a go

Remember that when you first started your old school, you didn't know you were going to love it so much and the same goes for your new one. It may be bigger and the subjects harder, but if you give yourself a chance to get used to the environment, you'll be surprised at how you might feel. If you're going to a more senior school it's important to remember everyone is going through the same change together.

I won't know anyone at my new school – I want my old friends back!

- A sea of new faces is difficult, especially if you've left a fabulous group of friends behind.
- It can help to think of making new friends as widening your social circle rather than replacing old ones (after all you still have your old friends).
- As the old saying goes – a stranger is just a friend you haven't met yet.

Find-a-friend tips

- Pretend you're not nervous even if you are.
- Smile a lot and act friendly to anyone who talks or smiles at you.

How to prepare yourself for a new school

- Look at the school website and check it out so you know what to expect in terms of the location, building, and feel of the school.
- Ask around. Someone you know will know someone who goes there. Ask them about the school and teachers.
- Take some familiar items with you (a pencil case, bag, or a favorite pen) so you have something to hang on to when you feel unsettled.

body changes and growing up

I don't want to be grown up. I don't want my body to change. How can I stop it happening?

You can't stop puberty. It's happening because your brain knows your body is ready to change and mature. The changes may make you feel unhappy and weird at first because everything will feel new and your **hormones** will be raging, but these changes are essential and in time you'll be glad they've happened.

I feel caught between being a teenager and a kid. One minute I want to be grownup and different, and the next I don't want anything to change.

- It's common to feel caught between two worlds during puberty. You might feel angry and sad that you don't quite fit into either.

- The important thing is not to rush the process or give yourself a hard time for feeling unhappy.

- Express how you feel to others and let yourself veer between the two until you're ready to be the new you.

Puberty – the physical changes to expect

- Height increase
- Weight increase
- Changes in body hair
- Skin changes, i.e. pimples

Emotional changes

- Mood swings: one minute you're happy, the next you're sad (blame your hormones).
- Feelings of confusion about wanting to be grown up and wanting to stay a child.
- Irritability and anxiousness.
- Many of us feel less confident during puberty – we need to get used to the new person we are, emotionally and physically.

Who said that?

"I felt awkward growing up because of my height. I was so much bigger than everyone else."

Michael Phelps, the greatest Olympian ever, stands tall at six feet four inches (1.95 m) and 198 pounds (90 kg)

emotional changes and loss

Change can happen in all kinds of ways. Sometimes this causes emotions that can be hard to deal with...

My best friend has fallen in love and has really changed. She's into clothes and make-up and flirting and I hate it. I want things to be the way they used to be.

- Even the deepest most secure friendships change and alter with time, because all our relationships react to the changes that are going on around us.
- Friends can't help falling in love, changing their interests, and growing away from the way they used to be.
- If you want your friendships to survive, the secret is to not hold tight to the past. Allow your friends to become the people who they want to be.

In the last year I've really lost who I am. I used to have no trouble doing well at school. Now I'm average and finding it hard to accept.

- Losing your confidence can happen more easily than you think, especially when you have been through a series of large changes such as changing schools, puberty, and new friendships.
- There is nothing wrong with being average but if you're falling behind or finding it hard, speak to your teacher about how to get back on track.
- What's important is not to assign yourself a loser label but to work on rebuilding your confidence. Focus on what will make you feel strong and successful again.

Emotional changes during your teen years

Change 1: You find yourself growing apart from friends you used to love being with.
How to deal with it: Accept that friendships change. Keep your old friends for memories, but don't be afraid to go out there and find new ones.

Change 2: You find yourself arguing with your parents when you used to get along.
How to deal with it: Understand this is part of the natural separation process that occurs as you get older. Show them you still love them and your relationship will survive.

Change 3: You find yourself wanting more privacy from siblings and parents.
How to deal with it: Ask others to respect your privacy and promise you will respect theirs.

Who said that?

"We just grew apart, so we're not friends anymore."

Nicole Ritchie on her best friend from childhood, Paris Hilton

changes at home

Changes at home come in a variety of shapes and sizes. Some are small and cause a ripple of anxiety. Others are large and can change everything.

I think my dad has lost his job because things have really changed at home. My parents fight about money a lot, and my dad seems sad, but no one's saying anything. What do I do?

- Money worries can change life at home in very real and difficult ways.
- The best way to cope is not to put on a happy face but to ask your parents to be truthful with you about what's going on.
- Ask what you can do to help.
- Tell your parents that not knowing the truth is making you anxious and upset.

My mom's started working again and I hate it. I liked it when she was there when I got back from school. Now, she seems so busy and is always too tired for me.

Having a parent change their role is hard, but the benefits often outweigh the initial problems.

1) Make sure you're being supportive to your mother so that when she gets home, she's not so busy with house stuff that she can't talk to you.

2) Tell her you miss her (without laying on the guilt). It's likely she's missing you too and you could both do with making some quality time for each other.

Signs something has changed at home

- You dread going home.
- There's a weird atmosphere.
- Your parents stop talking when you come into a room.
- Your parents pretend to be happy.
- Your parents argue more than usual.
- Your parents are always asking you to go to your room.

Did you know?

Financial pressures force mothers to work, despite more than two-thirds preferring to be at home with their children.

moving and emigrating

We're moving in two weeks and it's made me really sad. I was born here and I love it. I can't believe I have to leave it all behind.

We may not think it, but home is where the heart is. Where we live is embedded with a sense of deep security, which means moving can be a very painful and hard experience.

- Moving is upsetting, which is why it's listed amongst the top five stress outs of all time.

- Part of the problem is there is a huge sense of loss every time we leave a place that we've grown attached to.

- It's made even worse when you have to leave friends, family, and perhaps a parent behind, which is why you need to make the time to say your goodbyes, and allow yourself a period to feel sad before giving your new place a chance.

- Moving on is tough, but you can do it with small steps.

My family is **emigrating** to the Far East for my dad's job and I am so upset. I don't want to go but they won't leave me behind.

- You may think you'd like to stay without them, but losing your home and your family in one swoop would be more devastating than going along for the ride.
- Help yourself by researching where you're going so you know what to expect in terms of language, schools and weather.
- Make sure you find ways to keep in contact with friends back home. Instant messaging, social networking sites, and email all mean you can keep in contact as much as before. It's not the same, but it will make the adventure much easier.

Four ways to make moving abroad easier

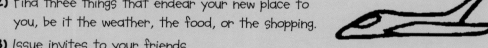

1) It's the chance for an adventure.

2) Find three things that endear your new place to you, be it the weather, the food, or the shopping.

3) Issue invites to your friends.

4) Bear in mind sometimes it's easier to leave, than be left behind.

It happened to me!

"I've moved seven times in the last five years thanks to my dad's job. It's hard leaving friends behind and starting new schools, but it's made me closer to my family. It's my family that's my security, not the building we live in."

Melissa, 15

parents separating

Whatever the reasons behind your parents' separation, it's essential to remember they are not separating from you, but from each other. Just understanding this can make coping with a family breakdown easier.

My dad's been gone for two weeks and though mom says he's away I know they have separated. I miss him a lot, what do I do?

Parents often make the mistake of not talking to their kids about what is happening. Thinking they want to protect you from the unpleasantness of the situation, but all they are doing is making it harder. Instead of going along with the pretence, talk to your mom and tell her what you know, explaining you need to speak to your father for your own peace of mind.

Ever since my parents separated last year I find myself crying and getting upset at the slightest thing. I never used to be like this.

- With the loss of all you knew and trusted, it's normal to experience feelings of sadness, tearfulness, and misery. All of these are a part of coping with all of the changes you and your family have had to deal with.

- Having said that, feeling so overwhelmed is also a sign you must talk to your parents about your feelings so they can start to reassure you that everything's going to be okay.

- Remember that not all parental separations lead to **divorce**. Separation is, for some couples, a time-out period to assess how to repair a relationship.

How a separation might make you feel

- Powerless
- Angry
- Upset
- Confused
- Depressed
- Shocked
- Anxious

It happened to me!

"My parents separated for nine months last year. At the time I knew they'd been arguing but didn't know what about. When I found out my dad had cheated I thought it was a divorce for sure. However, they went to counselling and now he's back and they are trying to work things out."

Matt, 12

divorce

Since my parents got divorced, nothing is the same and it makes me angry that I am paying for their decision. Will it always be this hard?

- Our parents are a vital source of our stability, which is why divorce can be a heart-wrenching experience and adversely affect everything in your world.
- The many changes that come with divorce are hard to accept all at once and though it may not seem like it now, life will get easier.
- Feeling angry with all you have lost is a part of the grieving process, but what's important is to admit to how you feel to your parents.
- If you can't talk to them, ask to speak to a counsellor who specializes in helping kids from divorced families. Your teacher may know of a good one. If not, ask your GP.

I feel guilty because I am relieved my parents have divorced but sad because we're not all together anymore.

It's natural to feel a mixture of relief and pain at your parent's divorce, especially if you've lived in an atmosphere of fights, violence, or verbal abuse.

Don't feel guilty, your feelings are an indication that you love your parents but are wise enough to know they are not suited to each other.

How a divorce might change your life

1) Who you live with – custody arrangements may mean you are only able to see your parents on certain days that were decided by the court

2) Where you live – you may have to move and you may have to change schools due to custody arrangements or money.

3) Relations with extended family – you may see less of one side of the family for a while.

4) Lifestyle changes – money may be short.

It happened to me!

"When my parents first got divorced things got worse before they got better. They were always saying nasty things about each other, and my mom was always questioning me about what my dad had bought for his house and telling me he was cheap. My dad kept asking me if mom was seeing anyone and I started to feel like I was expected to spy for them. One day I broke down and told my mom I couldn't handle it anymore – she talked to my dad and now they're really careful what they say to me."

Ben, 13

19

stepfamilies

My dad got remarried last year to a woman with two kids. Even after a year of spending weekends with them, I don't love them. I pretend we're one big happy family but I feel like a stranger and hate going there.

- Stepfamilies happen when parents remarry or start living with new partners. A new stepfamily can also mean learning to deal with **stepsiblings**, stepparents, and even stepgrandparents.

- While the pressure is there for you to be part of an instant perfect family, the reality is these people are strangers to you so you have to give yourself time to get to know them.

- This means lowering your expectations of how you're supposed to feel.

- You don't have to love them, or even like them, but it will pay off if you aim to fit in.

- If you're finding it especially hard, talk to your parents about how tough you're finding the changes.

I am desperate for my divorced parents to get back together but recently they both told me they had new partners. I feel gutted. I love the way life used to be when we were all together.

- As hard as it is, at some point you have to let go of how things used to be and stop hoping for the impossible.

- Divorce means your parents no longer want to be together, and legally are no longer considered to be man and wife.

- They have moved on, and while it may be the very last thing you want, it's already happened.

- By all means, treasure the memories you have from when you were all together, but remember your parents are still your parents even if you're no longer living as a complete family.

Changes that may happen when you have a stepfamily

1) A parent's surname may change, or there may be more people with your family name.

2) A parent may move further away or to a new home.

3) You may have to move homes and school if you're living with that parent.

4) You may have to get used to a different family dynamic, i.e. different house rules, chores, and bed routines.

5) You may find yourself sharing a room.

6) You may suddenly become an older or younger stepsibling.

7) You may have to eat different kinds of foods and be part of a different culture.

8) One parent may have less special time to spend with you.

How to get on with your stepparent

- Give them a chance – don't just decide you're going to hate them because your parents are no longer together.

- Be prepared to feel jealous and territorial about the parent they are with. It's normal but you need to work it through with your parent.

- Don't feel bad if you like them – it doesn't mean you're being disloyal to your other parent.

- Don't be mean – a stepparent is an easy target for your anger but that doesn't mean you can off load on them.

stepsiblings

Until my mom got married last year I was an only child but now I have an older stepsister and a baby half-brother. I'm finding it hard to deal with because my mom's never there for me anymore.

- A new baby is hard enough to deal with, but a new family and a stepsister to boot is a tough mix. On the one hand you have to deal with the loss of the family you knew and loved plus you have to deal with suddenly being part of a larger family with siblings.

- All siblings fight and argue, but with stepsiblings the chance of conflict is higher than usual because there is just so much more to cope with.

- The good news is everyone will be finding it hard to adjust so talk about how you feel.

- Your mom may not be able to give you the same amount of attention, but you should be able to find a compromise.

I'm really angry because I have to spend the holidays with my dad's new family who I haven't met yet. I don't want to go because I'll have to share a room and when my dad's at work I'll be with strangers.

It's normal to fear change and be angry that your life is being disrupted, which is why you have to call your dad and tell him you're feeling anxious about sharing a room and about the times when he's not going to be there. Ironing out these worries before you leave can help make the situation less frightening.

Helpful tip: If your parent can't understand what you're going through, remind them (as nicely as you can) that they chose their partner but you did not choose their partner's kids! Explain that to you it's like moving into a house with roomates that you don't know and didn't choose.

It happened to me!

"It took me a long time to get on with my stepsiblings. When I was 13 they were an easy target for all my anger about my parents' divorce and having to move school and house. I was too scared to get angry with my mom, so I took it out on them. Luckily my mom spotted what was happening and we worked it out. Now they are just my brother and sister. It's normal, just a family."

Leah, 18

living with an illness

Living with an ill parent, or living with your own illness, is frightening on a number of levels.

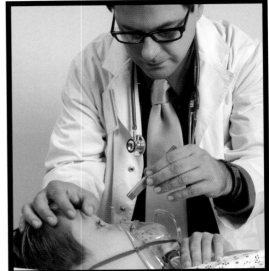

Aside from losing your old life, it's also about adapting to numerous and sometimes difficult changes.

My mom's really ill and I don't know what's wrong with her or how to deal with it. It's really scaring me but my dad just says, "Oh she's fine, don't worry."

- Adults often make the mistake of being overprotective, pretending everything is okay when you know it's not.

- What you have to do is not be part of the pretence but speak up and say you know something is wrong and you need to hear the truth. That will allow you to deal with what's really happening rather than guessing.

- Prepare yourself for any changes you mom's illness might cause. You might need to help out more at home for example. It may mean your mom is away or very tired when at home which could all mean you have less time to spend together as a family. The important thing is to help and support each other.

Different reactions

People respond differently to news of illness and have different ways of coping.

- Some cry and scream and shout.
- Others insist everything is going to be okay.
- Others pretend nothing has changed. It doesn't mean that they are unfeeling or dramatic just that they are behaving in a way that helps them cope.
- The important thing is to be open and honest about your feelings with your parents.

Patient tip

Try to understand what you have to do to manage your disease. It will help you to feel in control and less afraid.

I've been diagnosed with an illness that means I have to have an operation and stay in hospital for a while. My doctor told me I'd get better but would feel bad for a while. It's upset my mom and I don't want to make her cry again by asking her questions, but I don't understand what's happening to me.

- If you can't face talking to your parents for fear of upsetting them, ask your doctor to explain to you what's happening and why in simpler terms. It's your right to know.
- Also ask him if there is a support group available or a helpline you could ring, as these often have trained counsellors who can answer all your questions and give you some much needed support to deal with what's happening to you.
- Be honest about how much you want to know. Some people want to find out everything they can but some might find it too scary and limit the amount they want to know.

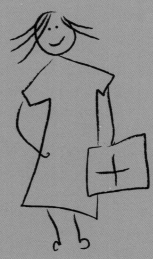

death of a grandparent

I can't believe my grandmother has gone. I miss her so much and cry every night but I don't want to upset my mom and tell her how I feel, so I say I am fine but inside I'm not.

The death of a grandparent may well be one of the first bereavements you will ever have to deal with.

- As well as your own pain you will have to deal with the pain your own parents are in.

- We protect our parents as much as they try to protect us, but when someone dies it pays to be honest about your feelings.

- Saying "I'm fine" sets up a precedent that will either stop parents and friends from checking you're okay (and so make you feel resentful and alone) or will make you bottle up your feelings and make you feel worse.

How can I help my mom get over my granddad's death? I hate seeing her so upset...

- Remember, nothing can make your mom feel better immediately. **Grief** can be a long process (see page 44).

- What does help is being around for your mom, and letting her know that you understand how she feels.

- Try to do more around the house. Even if all you do is put on the washing or make her some tea, it will help more than you think.

It happened to me!

"My grandmother died when I was on a school trip so I never had a chance to tell her how much I loved her, which really hurt. My mom suggested I write her a letter, which sounded stupid at first but when I got going I wrote three pages telling her how upset I was she was gone. It helped so much."

Chloe, 12

death of a parent

Losing a parent is the hardest thing you will ever go through. It's essential to find support and help.

I'm devastated my mom has two months left to live. I keep thinking if I'd behaved more or tried harder she'd be okay, and that somehow it's my fault. I love her so much. What can I do?

- When hope is taken away, it's natural to feel desperate and angry and even blame yourself (although logically you know that's not true). Remember, you haven't made this happen and can't fix it either.

- You may even find yourself making bargains in the hope that you can change the **inevitable**.

- What you can control is what you do with the time that's left. Make sure you spend quality time with your mom and that you say everything you need to

say about how you love her and what she means to you. It's important that when she is gone you have no regrets. This will help you cope.

- Make sure friends and teachers know what is going on so they can support you.

- Ask to see a counsellor who will have loads of advice on how to get through this.

- Treat yourself every day.

Create a memory box together

The idea is to create a treasure box that you can go to whenever you feel sad and alone. The box can be filled with anything you and your parent choose, for example:

- Special photographs
- Articles of clothing
- Jewelery
- DVDs and CDs
- Letters from your parent
- Postcards
- Information about your parent that you didn't know, such as their own childhood memories and hopes for you

- Stories about your birth
- Ideas/advice from your parent for your future

My dad suddenly died of a heart attack. I had no time to say goodbye or tell him I loved him.

- An unexpected death is as painful and difficult to deal with as an expected one.
- Which is why talking about the person who has died is one of the best ways to deal with what has happened.
- Remembering the ways in which the parent loved you and knew you loved them back is also important.

Famous people who lost a parent as a child

- Madonna lost her mother at the age of five.
- Prince William and Prince Harry lost their mother, Diana, Princess of Wales, when William was 15 and Harry was 12.

losing a friend

My best friend died of cancer four months ago. We'd been best friends since we were five years old and even though life has stayed the same, everything feels like it has changed.

People don't often realize that losing a friend is as upsetting an event as losing someone in your family. If it's happening to you, here's what you need to know.

- You may feel your life has drastically changed. This is because every day feels different without your friend.
- Small things from sitting in class to eating lunch can feel strange and difficult without your friend.
- On top of this is the feeling that life is no longer certain and safe.
- What you have to do is talk about what's happening with your parents and/or a counsellor so you can find a way through your grief.
- You may even feel guilty about carrying on without your friend and enjoying new friendships.

A friend was killed in an accident over the holidays. We weren't best friends but his death has really affected me. I feel really scared all the time and afraid of being alone.

- These feelings are more common than you think.
- The death of someone you know, especially in a tragic accident, brings to the surface all kinds of fears about being separated from loved ones and being hurt yourself.
- You need to talk to someone about your anxieties so they don't spiral out of control. Try a school counsellor, your parents, or a teacher at your school.

Grief is personal

There is no "right way" to react when someone dies and every person will respond differently. Don't let other people tell you what the right and wrong way to grieve is. Though grieving has its stages, you have to expereince them the way you feel is right for you. When you've lost someone it's important to:

1) Remember them at their best and what you loved about them.

2) Talk about them with other friends.

3) Look after yourself so that you feel you can cope with what has happened. This means eating well, trying to get some sleep, and exercising.

4) Remind yourself that though you're sad they're gone, they will live on in your memories.

coping with a funeral

Deciding whether or not to go to a funeral is hard and is dependent on many factors. What's important to realize is that you need to do what's right for you, not what people expect you to do.

It's my grandfather's funeral but I've never been to one before, and the thought is terrifying. I want to be there for him but don't know if I can cope.

- The best way to cope is to know what to expect.

- Talk to your parent about the details of the funeral. Is it a burial or a **cremation**, will the casket be open or closed, and will there be a religious ceremony and/or speeches by friends and family? What is expected of you and how long will the service be?

- The answers to these questions can help you to determine which parts of the funeral (if any) you want to attend.

My parents have decided to cremate my grandmother – it's horrible that they are doing this to her!

- It's likely a cremation was your grandmother's wish.
- Many people plan their own funerals and say what they want. For many, a cremation is what they feel most comfortable with.
- The idea may seem terrible, but remember your grandmother's body is dead and can no longer feel pain. Plus you will not see it happen and there is no smoke and no smell.
- Afterwards your parents will be given your grandmother's ashes, which they will either scatter in a special place or keep.

Quick quiz: should I go to the funeral?

1) Can you handle seeing the casket/coffin?   Yes/No
2) Will going help support another member of your family?   Yes/No
3) Is there a friend there to support you?   Yes/No
4) Is fear of breaking down holding you back?   Yes/No

Results
More than 2 "Yes"es – you should go
Less than 2 "Yes"es – you should stay home

Funeral etiquette

1) Do I have to wear black?
Not necessarily. Ask your parents what they feel you should wear and/or tell them what you want to wear. Some people feel they want to wear something brighter than black to celebrate not mourn a person's life.

2) What do I say to people?
If you're going to a friend's funeral or a relative, all you have to say to the mourning family is, "I'm so sorry for your loss." If people are saying that to you, all you need say back is, "Thank you."

3) How long do I have to stay?
This is completely up to you. If you feel you're coping stay as long as you want. If you feel horrible, out of your depth, and in need of privacy, tell whoever you are with that you need to leave.

4) What about religion?
It's up to you what you believe, but if you are going to a funeral that has a religious slant different from yours, then you need to respect that and abide by the right etiquette (ask friends and family what you need to do).

grief – dealing with loss

When someone dies you will experience an intense feeling of sorrow called grief. This process helps you accept a deep loss and find a way to carry on with your life.

My mom died three weeks ago and I haven't cried yet. My aunt says I am being weird but I just feel so angry. What's wrong with me?

- Everyone experiences grief differently. While films might show people weeping and wailing, you may find yourself numb to everything or feeling more angry than sad.

- This is because there is a whole range of feelings within grief. Despair, sadness, guilt, relief and fear are all part of the process and you may feel yourself swaying violently from one to the other as you grieve.

- Don't let others dictate how you should feel. It's your pain and you should deal with it in the most honest way possible.

How am I ever going to get over losing my dad?

- It's a cliché to say it but time really does heal. While you will always miss your father, you won't always feel so much pain when you think about him.
- Allow yourself to go through the grief process of: numbness, yearning, anger, depression, and acceptance (see page 44).
- Ensure you talk to your family, especially your mom. Many people benefit from seeing a bereavement counselor who will advise you on how to cope.

How to cope with grief

1) Ask for help and support.

2) Try to find a way to express whatever you are feeling, if not vocally then try writing it down.

3) Give yourself time to grieve – don't fill your time so you can't think.

4) Don't try to rush the process – it will be over when it's over.

5) Keep reminding yourself that things will get easier.

6) Talk to someone else who has lost someone.

Physical effects of grief

1) Sleep problems – it's common to sleep too little or too much.

2) Eating problems – you may lose your appetite or feel hungry all the time.

3) Headaches – you may feel a tight band round your head – known as a tension headache.

4) Feeling ill with mysterious aches and pains – also common but get yourself checked out by your doctor.

5) Bouts of non-stop crying – completely normal. They will stop when you feel ready.

depression versus sadness

My mom died six months ago and I miss her a lot. I thought I'd be over my grief by now but the sadness has come back. What's wrong with me?

- With a major life change and a significant loss, you are bound to feel intense sadness. Sometimes it can feel like you are stuck feeling that way. If you cannot shift the feelings and they are bringing you down, it is essential to seek help so you can move on.

- Though there are five stages (see page 44) to grief you may find yourself going through the steps several times and may even find one recurs more than the others.

- It's completely normal and is only a problem if you begin to feel stuck.

- A sign that your sadness is a more deep-rooted depression is if you cry all the time, feel depressed for days at a time, can't bring yourself to find joy in anything, feel lethargic and can see no hope at all in your life. If this is the case you need to seek help.

My mom hasn't been able to cope with anything since my dad died a year ago. For the last year I have struggled to look after my younger brother, pay bills, shop and cook, as all she does is cry and stay in bed. I haven't told anyone because I don't want to be disloyal.

- It sounds like your mother is depressed and needs help.
- It's not disloyal to reach out for someone when they are unable to. Your dad would want you to do this, especially as so much has been resting on your shoulders.
- Talk to a relative, family friend, or a friend's mother about what's happening.

Sadness is...

- Feeling upset when you think of the person you have lost
- Crying when you think of them
- Feeling you're never going to stop missing them
- Feeling there is a huge hole in your life

A deep-rooted depression is...

- Feeling there is no hope
- Feeling unable to do anything that's part of your normal life
- Feeling stuck for a long time in one place
- Feeling you can't go on

who to talk to

Ever since my mom died my friends have been avoiding me. One friend even crossed the road when she saw me coming. I desperately need someone to talk to but I feel so alone.

- Finding the right person to talk to can be a challenge at times of deep loss, but there are a variety of places and people you can turn to.
- Friends and adults can react badly to a death and many don't know what to say.
  - Some imagine that they'll say the wrong things and just make a bad situation worse and others feel you're likely to want to be alone.
  - This is why it can help to tell friends what you need from them. Perhaps a night out forgetting things, or a chance to open up. If that doesn't work seek support from an alternative source.
  - Consider relatives, an online support group (see page 48) or your doctor. All these people can listen and help you, if you let them.

My doctor has suggested I see a bereavement therapist – what's that?

- Bereavement counsellors and therapists are experts in helping people cope with their grief
- They can help if, for example, you find you're stuck in a deep sadness or anger months after losing someone.
- Their work is completely confidential and many people find it's a relief to open up and say whatever they want to someone knowing that it won't be held against them.

People to turn to for support

- Help lines
- Online support groups
- Relatives
- Teachers
- A friend's parent
- Peer support groups

Helpful tip

Let people who care about you take care of you, even if you're determined to show you're coping and are strong. We all need looking after now and again.

helping a friend cope with change

My friend lost her dad and I am going to see her next week. I don't know what to say or do – help!

- A death of someone you love is a lonely and frightening experience and once the initial support and funeral is over, many people feel abandoned and alone, which is where it can pay to be a supportive friend.
- The first thing to do is behave naturally and then just say you're sorry for her loss.
- You could ask her how she is and if there is anything you can do to help, or simply just sit with her.
- If she starts talking about her dad, talk normally to her, if not, don't feel in a rush to fill the silence.
- Sometimes all grieving people want is company and someone close to hold their hand when they get upset. Your support can be shown just by being there for your friend.

My friend lost her mom to an accident a year ago. Recently she's admitted to me that she feels life is over and not worth living anymore, but has begged me not to tell her dad. She's frightening me – what do I do?

- Sometimes helping someone and being a good friend means speaking for them when they can't.
- This means telling someone in a position to help your friend.
- Feeling suicidal from grief is a sign your friend is in deep distress and needs help from both her father and a professional such as a doctor or therapist.

How to be a good friend

DO learn to listen.

DO give them a hug if you feel they need it.

DO cry with them if you're upset.

DO bear in mind that certain times of the year will be hard for them (Christmas and birthdays etc).

DON'T jump in with platitudes such as "They are in a better place."

DON'T say, "I know how you feel."

DON'T change the subject just because you find it difficult.

DON'T be afraid to say, "I don't know" if they ask you something.

making change work for you

I feel guilty because I have started to feel happy again after losing my mom two years ago. Sometimes whole days go by when I don't think of her and then I feel so bad for having a good time when she can't.

- The good news is that the end result of change is that something new happens, whether it's a chance to become someone new or be somewhere new or both.

- Feeling guilty is 100% normal. Every time you experience these feelings try and remember that being happy is what a loved one would want for you.

- A parent, friend or relative wouldn't want you to grieve for them forever.

- Parents in particular would want you to go on and live a full and happy life full of laughter.

- If you're not going to do it for yourself, then do it for them.

It happened to me!

"Moving to London was the worst day of my life. When we arrived it was cold and wet. I hated our new house, missed my friends and was so angry with my parents for moving that I couldn't speak to them for days. On my first day at school I was determined to hate it. However, when my dad dropped me off at my new school he said, "Change is your chance to reinvent yourself Amy," and suddenly I realized he was right. I had the chance to be anyone I wanted, a new and improved me, a better version of the old me, or someone different. It was totally liberating."

Amy 15

How to deal with change

1) Don't let others tell you how to cope. The best way to cope is to find your own method, whether that's dealing with it slowly, quickly, or ignoring it for now.

2) Remind yourself that you'll get through this because you will.

3) Give yourself time – it's a cliché but it's true. Things will get better and by this time next year you'll be in a different place.

4) Getting over a life change doesn't mean forgetting the past, it means accepting it and choosing to move on.

The lessons change and loss teach you

1) It proves who you are by showing:

- What matters to you
- That you are brave
- That you are stronger and more resilient

2) It makes you appreciate the people in your life and reminds you:

- Not to take them for granted
- To tell them you love them

the five stages of grief

Dr. Elisabeth Kübler-Ross, an expert in the grief associated with death and dying, pioneered the five stages of grief. The five stages can be linked to any kind of loss, no matter how big or small, and they can help you to understand not only what's happening to you, but also how your feelings are completely natural and normal. Bear in mind that the cycles can be repeated within one episode of grief, and that there is no timescale to each stage. Also, you may not follow the stages in this exact order. Everyone is different.

Stage 1 – Denial

This is a refusal to accept what has happened. This is our body's defense mechanism and a way of dealing with shock. You may feel numb or simply refuse to believe what you have been told. If you have suffered bereavement, you may even imagine you see the person you have lost in crowds.

Stage 2 – Anger

You may find yourself angry with a person who is ill or dying, angry with yourself or just angry about everything. You may take it out on the people close to you or turn it inwards. It's this stage that frightens off many people who want to help, so it can help to know this if a friend is suffering from grief.

Stage 3 – Bargaining

This is the stage where you try to make deals with yourself or God (or whatever you believe in), and promise all kinds of things if only life would go back to normal. It's a frightening stage because when it ends you start to realize that you have no control over what's happening.

Stage 4 – Sadness

A period of deep sadness, low moods and regret, as the reality of what's happening begins to sink in. You may find you can't find any joy in life anymore, and start to imagine nothing will ever be better again. Your eating patterns and sleep may be dramatically affected and you may need to seek help from your doctor.

Stage 5 – Acceptance

The stage when you finally come to terms with the trauma that's occurred and accept that life has changed, perhaps forever. You don't forget what has happened. You just carry on and realize that, for now, the grieving is over.

glossary

cremation A process whereby the body of someone who has died is reduced to ash through a heat process. The ash is then usually scattered somewhere special or kept by the remaining family

divorce The legal termination of a marriage and means the couple in question are no longer seen as related in the eyes of the law

emigrating When a person leaves the country of their birth and goes to live in another

funeral The ceremony held before the burial or cremation of a dead person.

grief The emotional process by which we come to terms with a loss

hormones Chemicals that help control growth and other body processes

inevitable Something that cannot be avoided or escaped

security Protection from harm

separation A separation is when a married couple decides they no longer want to live together, but decide to live apart for a while to try and resolve their differences

stepsibling A brother or sister who is related to you by marriage i.e. the children of your stepmother or stepfather

further information

Caring Connections
www.caringinfo.org
Helpline: 800.658.8898
Living with an illness and
grief support

The Dougy Centre
For Grieving Children and Families —
www.dougy.org
The Dougy Center was the first
center in the United States to
provide peer support groups
for grieving children.

Hospice
www.hospicenet.org
Information, help and support for
families, children and teens.

index

Printed in the U.S.A. — CG